CONTENTS

USEFUL WORDS

Orbit
the circular path taken by an object around a planet or moon without landing on it

Satellite
a robot spacecraft that orbits the Earth

Spacecraft
the machine you live inside when in space

Astronaut/ Cosmonaut
a person who flies in space

Mission Control
the team of people on Earth who help you during your mission

WHAT IS SPACE?

We all live on a planet called Earth that travels through space around our star, which is called the Sun.

The Solar System

The Earth is one of nine planets orbiting the Sun – Mercury, Venus, Earth, Mars, Jupiter, Saturn, Uranus, Neptune and Pluto. Some of these planets have moons orbiting them. Between Mars and Jupiter there is a belt of millions of large rocks called 'asteroids'. All together, this is called the Solar System.

Earth!

This illustration shows our Solar System – you can see how small Earth is compared to the other planets.

This is one of many galaxies, called the Great Nebula.

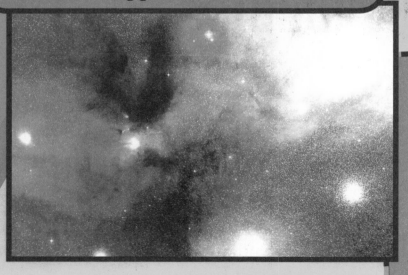

How big is space?

The Universe is made up of hundreds of galaxies. The Sun is just one of thousands of stars that make up our galaxy, and the stars we see in the night sky may have their own planets orbiting them.

Space is BIG!

If you think of the Sahara Desert in Africa as the Universe, then our Solar System would be just one grain of sand in that whole desert!

Getting into space

To get into space you need a rocket, which burns fuel out of the nozzles at the back and pushes itself and the spacecraft up into space.

Parts of the rocket are brought together and prepared weeks before the launch. The completed rocket stands on its tail on the launch pad. The clocks timing the trip count backwards to zero (countdown), then the engines fire and you climb into the sky (a launch). Soon, the sky turns from blue to black and you are in space.

Getting home again

As the spacecraft re-enters the Earth's atmosphere it becomes white-hot. The heat prevents the astronauts talking to Ground Control on their radio, but a heat shield keeps them safe and cool inside. By bouncing through the atmosphere like a stone skimming across water, the spacecraft can slow down enough to land by parachute or, as a Space Shuttle does, like an aeroplane on a runway.

Gravity

The Earth spins, creating gravity, which keeps us on the ground and makes things fall if we drop them. On Earth, gravity is measured at 1G.

There is no gravity in space, so inside a spacecraft everything floats – including you. This is called 'zero-G' (G = gravity) or 'weightlessness'.

A view of the Earth from the Moon, where gravity is $\frac{1}{6}$ G.

WHAT IS AN ASTRONAUT?

Astronauts often use desolate places on Earth to practise their skills.

'Astronaut' means 'star traveller'. In Russia, space explorers are called 'cosmonauts', which means the same thing. It takes a lot of work to become an astronaut or a cosmonaut.

Astronauts needed!

The first people in space were the air force's best test pilots. Today they ask for scientists, engineers and even teachers, depending on the purpose of the mission (the reason for the spaceflight).

Who's who on board

Commander
The person in charge of the crew

Crew
The team of astronauts chosen to fly a mission

Payload Specialists
The scientists who do the experiments

Mission Specialists/ Flight Engineers
The astronauts who look after the spacecraft itself

Training

Astronaut training takes a long time. Sometimes, an astronaut trains for years without ever flying in space. Others only get to make one spaceflight.

This photograph shows astronauts training in a huge water tank, to get used to working in a weightless environment (zero-G).

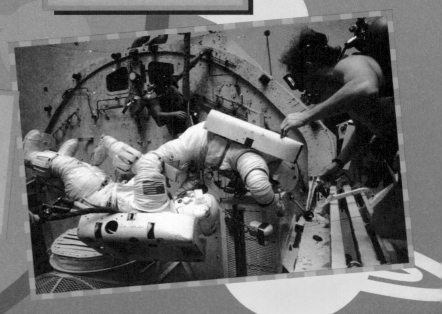

Roller-coaster ride

To learn how to cope in zero-G, astronauts practise in a special aircraft, known as the 'Vomit Comet', that flies up and down steep curves. For about 30 seconds at the top of the curve, those inside become weightless before the downward slope brings back gravity and they do it all over again. With up to 40 curves each flight, the plane can make you feel very ill, so don't have a large breakfast!

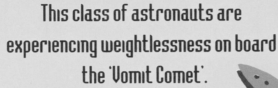

This class of astronauts are experiencing weightlessness on board the 'Vomit Comet'.

Design your own emblem here.

This is an emblem designed by the crew before a flight on the Space Shuttle Columbia.
 The main picture shows what the mission is for and the names of the crew go round the outside.

5

WAKEY, WAKEY

In space, astronauts are normally woken up by a favourite song or message from Mission Control on Earth. These are called 'wake-up calls' and are usually loud.

Washing

Because there's no gravity, there are no sinks or baths in space – the water would not stay in the bowl! Astronauts use a water gun, like a garden hose, and spray water on to soapy towels. Then they rub themselves all over to wash.

Hair care

Many astronauts keep their hair short as it is easier to look after. Astronauts with long hair have a full mop of floating hair in space.

Hair wash

You wash your hair by putting shampoo on your head and then firing the water gun at it. You rub your head to mix the shampoo and water, and rinse it clean with the water gun and a towel. And you don't use a hair dryer – you blow-dry your hair with hot air from the air conditioning hose. . .

Toilet trouble

Going to the toilet in space can be an interesting experience. With no gravity to make everything fall into the pan, the astronauts have to use a toilet with vacuum suction to draw waste down into a storage area. To get rid of liquid waste, the astronauts 'go' into a special tube that takes the liquid away into a container. The liquid is later dumped overboard into space where it shines in the sun like millions of stars, then evaporates.

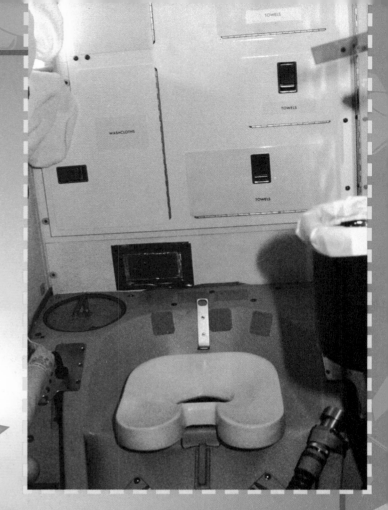

The problem with the toilet is that if the suction is too strong you can't get off the seat! If it is not strong enough, the next person may find a nasty surprise floating in mid-air. However, this is better than the early days of space travel when astronauts had to use plastic bags with very sticky tape on the top. This stuck to their bottoms so hard that it pulled the hair off when they tried to take it off! They had to seal the bag with a special tablet inside to prevent gases building up and exploding the bag a couple of days later!

Astronauts brush their teeth with special edible toothpaste. They can't spit the toothpaste out, so they have to swallow it when they have finished.

FEELING HUNGRY?

The food taken into space today is very different from that taken on early flights, when it was kept in tubes like toothpaste or sealed dry in small packs. Nowadays, the food is much more like it is at home.

A Russian cosmonaut prepares a meal on board the Space Shuttle Discovery.

Just like home

On short flights there is fresh fruit, bread, fruit juice and even sweets. On longer flights there is freeze-dried food, which is prepared by adding water.

Astronauts choose their food on Earth and label it so they know what to eat each day. As there are astronauts from many countries, a great variety of food is available — French cheeses, German cold meats, Russian soups and Asian curries.

Taking turns

Meal times give the crew a chance to relax together. Usually each crew member takes a turn to prepare the food for all the others. The food comes in trays. The base of the tray serves as a bowl and is covered by a see-through lid. There is hot and cold water and an oven for warming food.

Table manners

Astronauts do not sit at a table – they float in mid-air with their food attached to a tray. The tray can be stuck on the wall or on their leg to stop it floating away. Most of the food is moist and sticks to the knife and fork. They have to drink through straws that have a stopper to make sure no liquid leaks out.

The crew of Russia's Mir Space Station enjoying a meal.

Food fun

Astronauts can have great fun with food – eating with no hands as the food floats about. When drinks like orange juice float free in space they form a perfect ball, and touching it sends it spinning like a tiny orange planet. You have to take care, though, otherwise the liquid hits you in the face!

Some special food packaging used in space is also used on Earth, e.g. vacuum- or foil-packaging, freeze-dried food, sealed drinks with straws. Make up a menu of astronauts' food for a day. Remember that it should come in these special packs.

Breakfast	
Lunch	
Supper	

ALL IN A DAY'S WORK

Astronauts conduct experiments to see how things behave in zero-G. They often take photographs of their experiments and of the view of the Earth and the stars. Looking out of the window at Earth is one of the astronauts' favourite jobs.

Lost property

Many things are lost because an astronaut lets go of something that is not tied down. The flow of air around the spacecraft means the first place to look for lost things is in the air vents.

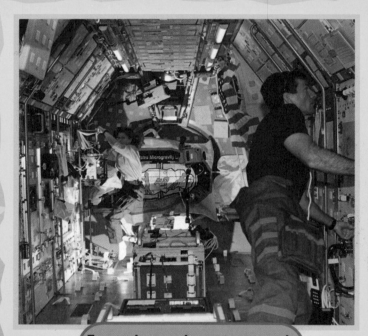

Two astronauts carrying out research. These astronauts were in space for 16 days, orbiting the Earth.

Astronauts do not have tables, or even chairs. Most of their working area is flat against the walls. To keep things such as pens, books and cameras in place, the astronauts use elastic straps or a special sticky patch called Velcro. If they wish to stay in one place for a long time, they can put their feet into loops on the floor and curl their toes to stop themselves floating away.

DROP PHYSICS MODULE

Moving moments

Astronauts usually work in groups, and while some are working in one part of the spacecraft, others are preparing a meal or sleeping.

Sometimes the spacecraft needs to be moved. If you are floating in the science labs or asleep when the spacecraft moves, you will stay still and the spacecraft wall will come to hit you! So the crew always try to move the spacecraft when everyone knows what is going to happen.

One of the astronauts having forty winks after a hard day's work aboard the Space Shuttle Challenger.

Time keeping

On Earth, we measure time according to the movements of the Earth around the Sun. We wake up in the morning (sunrise) and work in the daylight until we go to bed at night (after sunset).

In space, the astronauts go round Earth once every 90 minutes and see 17 sunrises and sunsets each day. They usually follow a clock set to their time at home on Earth.

This is the Spacelab Life Sciences laboratory module on board the Space Shuttle Columbia. You can see the tunnel-like passageway leading to the lab from the main part of the shuttle. On this particular mission, six astronauts and a vet spent two weeks in Earth orbit, carrying out medical research.

SCIENCE IN SPACE

Experiments conducted on spacecraft tell us not only about space, but also about ourselves and our planet.

This is Arabella, one of three common spiders taken on board the Skylab space station. She still managed to spin her web in zero-G!

Animal astros

Astronauts have taken insects into space to see how they fly without gravity and most of them just tumble in the air, confused. They need gravity to point themselves the right way.

Studies on some frogs, which have similar types of ear parts as humans, show how balance can be affected by taking away gravity; and rats and mice are used for research into human hearts.

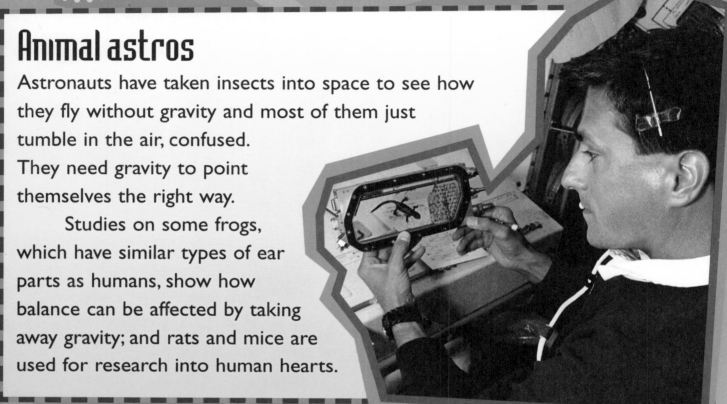

Light matters

When fish were taken up in sealed tanks, some of them swam upside down. When the astronauts shone lights on the top of the tank, the fish turned over and swam like they would on Earth. When heat lamps are used on plants, they grow towards the lamp. This shows that light and heat, as well as gravity, tell plants and animals which way is up or down.

These plants were grown on board the Space Shuttle Columbia.

Space study

Astronauts also study space itself. They record measurements from the Sun, planets and stars, take samples of the space environment and study the Earth's atmosphere.

Space medicine

Scientists in space can make medicines more safely and cleanly than on Earth. They also 'grow' crystals for use in computers and other machines.

This odd photograph was taken just as a liquid ball of water floated past the astronaut's face, making his eye look peculiar.

Imagine that you are an astronaut. Describe an experiment that you would like to perform in zero-G.

....

....

....

....

....

SPACE TECHNOLOGY

The technology used in space has come a long way since the early days.

from suit to Shuttle

When man first went into space, the spacecraft were so small that the astronauts wore them almost like suits. Now up to eight people can fly into space in comfort on one spacecraft.

The Shuttle is partly reusable – both the Orbiter, which carries the crew, and the rocket booster-tanks are used again. But the orange fuel tank is destroyed in re-entering the atmosphere. Scientists are now developing a totally reusable spacecraft that will fly from a runway into space and land back on the runway at the end of its mission.

Stations in space

In 1971 Russia launched the first of its seven *Salyut* space stations. These were replaced by *Mir* in 1986, in which cosmonauts from many countries could work together in space. The American space station *Skylab* flew in 1973 and 1974 and allowed astronauts to live in space for up to 84 days. The Russians could stay in space in *Salyut* and *Mir* for over a year.

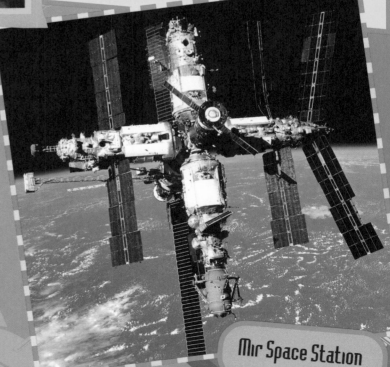

Mir Space Station

14

Looking ahead

Currently 16 space-exploring countries of the world are working together to build a huge International Space Station (ISS). There will be 45 launches from America, Russia, Japan and Europe in order to assemble the space station from over 100 parts. Over 75 spacewalks are planned totalling more than 1000 hours outside the spacecraft. It will take five years to build and will stay in space for the next 30 years.

The Space Shuttle Atlantis launches another spacecraft, destined for the planet Venus.

Design your own spacecraft and give it a name.

Astronauts give their spacecraft nicknames ('callsigns') which they use to identify themselves over the radio. The Shuttles are called *Columbia*, *Discovery*, *Endeavour* and *Atlantis* after famous ships. Astronauts also use the names of rivers, mountains, stars and even birds, but they have also used fun names too, including *Spider*, *Gumdrop*, even *Snoopy* and *Charlie Brown* after the cartoon characters.

SPACE SPIN-OFFS

What we have learned from going into space helps us every day on Earth. The things we get from space flights are called space spin-offs.

Satellites

Most of us watch TV without even realising that the pictures we see from around the world are beamed from satellites in orbit. Weather forecasters use data from weather satellites, and ships, aeroplanes and explorers use navigation satellites to pinpoint where they are.

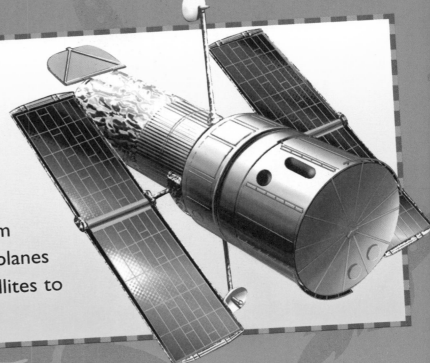

Space-age kitchen

Microwaves, foil-packed food and drink and non-stick saucepan coatings are just some of the things developed from space technology. Spacesuit coolant is now used in fridges and in equipment for sports injuries. Long-life food, freeze-dried meals and sports drinks with straws attached are all on astronauts' menus.

Technology

Computer technology used in the space programme has brought us home computers, the Internet, mobile phones, CDs and videos, as well as satellite TV stations. Medical advances include micro (key-hole) surgery, robot surgery (bionics) and plastic surgery.

Space-age wardrobe

The skills developed for making spacesuits are now used in survival and rescue clothing, as well as sportswear such as training shoes. Thick insulated shoes come from moonboots, and silver heat-retaining blankets come from astronaut survival kits.

Environmental concerns

From orbit, cameras can look down on the spreading of disease among forests and crops, and can also track damaging storms, forest fires, volcanoes and air pollution. Astronauts on board space stations have actually guided fishing fleets to shoals of fish, saving time and money. The effects of global warming, drought, flooding and erosion of coastlines are traced year by year from all sorts of spacecraft.

This photo was taken from the Mir space station while it was docked to the Shuttle Atlantis. Miles below you can see the west coast of America.

ROOM	ITEMS FOUND
Kitchen	
Living room	
Bedroom	
Bathroom	

Go into each of these rooms in your house and try to find at least one item in each room that has been developed from space technology.

BODY CHANGES

On Earth your frame of bones and muscles helps you stand and move against the pull of gravity. Without gravity, certain changes happen to your body. These can be good or bad, depending on how long you spend in space.

Motion sickness

Have you ever been in a boat on a rough sea, and felt sick? This is called 'motion sickness', and it happens because part of your body's balancing system senses movement and signals to your brain that you are not the right way up. Motion sickness affects many astronauts for their first few days in space until they get their 'space legs'.

Changing size

Your body is made up of a lot of fluids, though you only see skin and muscles. In space, fluids move around the body, and the waist of an astronaut gets thinner. Also, the spine relaxes and stretches so you grow up to 5cm taller. You return to normal size when you go back to Earth.

Red faces

Because your muscles do not need as much blood as they would on Earth, your brain thinks there is a problem and asks the heart for more blood as a safety measure. This means astronauts' faces look fatter and redder than usual. Their eyes also look puffy and sore.

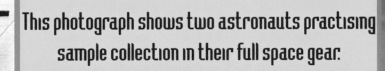
This photograph shows two astronauts practising sample collection in their full space gear.

Keeping fit

The longer you spend in space, the weaker your heart and bones become. To stop this, astronauts exercise in space every day. They use running tracks, which are fitted with straps to stop them floating off, rowing machines and exercise bikes.

Because you float in space, so does everything inside you. Astronauts have said that even though you can eat normally, your stomach feels full all the time.

Eyesight and hearing are normal. Talking is the same too, though you may sound as if you have a cold.

Draw a picture of yourself normally; then draw a picture of what you think you might look like in space.

ON EARTH

IN SPACE

OUT AND ABOUT

Sometimes astronauts need to work outside the spacecraft. To do this, they have to wear a special suit.

A suit for space

A spacesuit is a completely sealed set of clothes that holds in the air an astronaut needs to breathe. Helmets, gloves and boots are locked on to the main suit. When astronauts work outside they need a lot of information to hand. The latest helmets have a TV-like display, so the astronauts can read the information they need but still look through it to the outside. The helmets also have headlamps, and radio sets to let them talk to each other. Gloves are a problem because, inside them, astronauts lose the sense of touch. New gloves are currently being developed with sensors on the palms and fingertips to let the astronauts 'feel' what they are holding.

Problem solving

Astronauts have a drink supply in the suit. Sometimes this leaks and the astronaut gets a surprise orange juice shampoo! The astronauts can't get back inside to go to the toilet, so they wear a modern nappy and 'go' in the suit. It's hard to see what is behind you, so the suits have mirrors on the arms. There is even a rough patch of material inside the helmet that you can rub your itchy nose on!

Staying cool

To keep an even body temperature, the astronaut wears underwear covered in small tubes that pump water round the body. Temperatures in the sunlight can be as hot as an oven, while in the shade it can be as cold as a freezer.

It usually takes a few people to get you into your outdoor suit!

In space, you do not wear a suit, but float inside it.

Walking on the Moon

Spacesuits allowed us to walk on the Moon, which has $\frac{1}{6}$ the gravity of Earth, so it looks and feels like walking in slow motion. Some astronauts tried to jump high or throw things as if they were competing in a lunar Olympic Games.

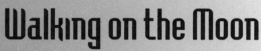

Space firsts

★ You probably know that the first man to walk on the Moon was **Neil Armstrong**, but here are a few more space firsts that you may not know.

★ The first man in space was a Russian called **Yuri Gagarin**.

★ The first American to go round the Earth was **John Glenn**, who many years later flew again on the Space Shuttle aged 77!

★ The first woman in space was again Russian, **Valentina Tereshkova**.

★ The first American woman in space was **Sally Ride**.

★ The first man to perform a spacewalk was **Alexei Leonov**.

★ The first British astronaut was **Helen Sharman**.

AT THE END OF THE DAY

At the end of a hard working day, the crew look forward to a good night's sleep. On most flights, astronauts go to sleep at the same time.

One of the astronauts gazes at Earth through a viewing port on board the Space Shuttle Atlantis.

Time out

Most of their time in space is packed full of things to do, but the crew do get some time off. On long flights, astronauts often talk to their families over the radio. Ground Control read out the news and the sports results as the crew eat the final meal of the day. Music tapes, books and videos are on board, and some astronauts even take musical instruments with them.

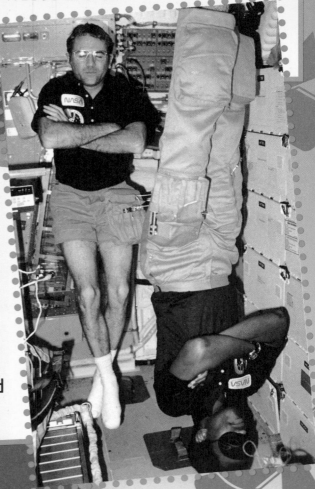

Turn the light off!

Because the lights stay on in the spacecraft nearly all the time and sunlight shines in the windows for up to 45 minutes every orbit, the windows have shades and the crew use sleep masks to keep the light out. They also wear earplugs to block out the noise of the spacecraft. Even when most things are turned off, the air fans still have to blow air around.

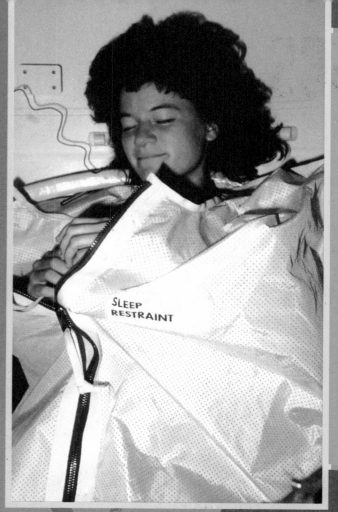

SLEEP RESTRAINT

floating beds

Early crews slept in their seats, but the Shuttle and the space stations have sleeping bags called sleep restraints. You can either strap them to the wall or float in them. You have to remember to tuck your arms in as they float in front of you. Waking up with two hands floating in front of your face can give you a surprise! Astronauts say they sleep normally in space but they miss putting their head on a pillow or feeling sheets on top of them. So straps tighten in and allow them to feel as though they are in bed.

There's even time to celebrate birthdays in space!

Write a list of all the special items you would take with you into space. Maybe you have some books, CDs or pictures that would remind you of home.

TOP

....
....
....
....
....

USEFUL ADDRESSES

National Aeronautics and
Space Administration (NASA)
Office of Public Affairs
NASA Headquarters
300 E. Street
SW Washington DC 20546
USA
Internet address:
http://www.nasa.gov

Write to an astronaut –
if you know the astronaut's
name send your letter to:
Code B
NASA LBJ Space Center
Houston
Texas 77058
USA

Write to a cosmonaut –
if you know the cosmonaut's
name send your letter to:
Cosmonaut Office
Yuri Gagarin Training Centre
(TsPK)
Zvyozdny
Gorodok (Star City)
Moscow
RUSSIA

Midlands Spaceflight Society Internet address:
http://homepages.infoseek.com/wemfas/midlands.html

European Space Agency
Postal address:
ESA Public Relations Service
8-10 rue Mario Nikis
75738 Paris 15
FRANCE
Internet address:
http://www.esrin.esa.it

Space Education Council
6 Borough Road
Kingston upon Thames
Surrey KT2 6BD
ENGLAND
Internet address:
http://www.kingston.ac.uk/sec/sechome.htm

British National Space Centre
151 Buckingham Palace Road
London SW1W 9SS
ENGLAND
Internet address:
http://www.bnsc.gov.uk

Science Museum, London
Exploration of Space
Gallery
Exhibition Road
South Kensington
London SW7 2DD
Internet address:
http://www.nmsi.ac.uk

National Space Science
Centre
Mansion House
41 Guildhall Lane
Leicester LE1 5FR
ENGLAND
Internet address:
www.nssc.co.uk

British Interplanetary Society
27-29 South Lambeth Road
London SW8 1SZ
ENGLAND
Internet address:
http://freespace.virgin.net/bis.bis/BIS.htm

British Astronomical Association
Burlington House
Piccadilly
London W1V 9AG
ENGLAND
Internet address:
http://www.ast.cam.ac.uk/~baa

Hubble Space Telescope
Internet address:
http://www.stsci.edu